THE *little* BOOK OF

60

Aubrey Malone

www.booksbyboxer.com

Published in the UK by
Books By Boxer, Leeds, LS13 4BS
© Books By Boxer 2015
All Rights Reserved

ISBN: 9781909732025

Yahoo!
At last you're

60

DON'T WORRY!!!
**Here's some expert advice
to help you get through it!**

I'm not sixty.
I'm **sexty**!

(Dolly Parton on
her 60th birthday)

By the time you reach 60, lots of body parts are larger than they used to be. Especially your tattoos.

(Greg Tamblyn)

I've become a pensioner.
I'm saving up for my
hospital trolley!

(Tom Baker)

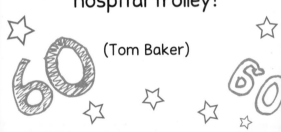

60 ☆ ☆ ☆ *60*

☆ Mickey Rooney has to ☆
live to be 100 so he
☆ can pay the alimony he ☆
owes all those ex wives.
He's not ALLOWED to die.

(George Burns)

I'm pleased to be here. Let's face it, at my age, I'm pleased to be anywhere.

(Ronald Reagan)

My wife is 60. I'd like to exchange her for two 30 year olds.

(Leopold Fechtner)

Exercise at 60? If we were meant to exercise at 60, God would have put jewellery on the floor.

(Joan Rivers)

60 ☆ ☆

☆ ☆

☆ I've been around so
long I knew Doris Day
before she was a virgin. ☆

(Groucho Marx)

No woman in the history of the world ever admitted she married a man for his money. How come I never saw a 17 year old girl with a 60 year old man who drives a truck?

(George Burns)

When my parents got to 60, they moved to Florida. They didn't want to, but this is America and hey, it's the law.

(Jerry Seinfeld)

60

I can't see myself putting make-up on my face at 60, but I **can** see myself going on a camel train to Samarkand.

(Glenda Jackson)

When I started in show business, the Dead Sea was only sick.

(George Burns)

My Dad's pants kept creeping up on him as the years went on. By 65 he was just a pair of pants and a head.

(Jeff Altman)

I have no views. When one is retired it is sensible to refrain from having views.

(Joseph Alsop)

I'll never make the
mistake of being
sixty again.

(Sid Caesar)

The greatest advantage of having babies in your sixties, is the fact that you can both be in nappies at the same time.

(Sue Kolinsky)

60

Being 60 means you get tired brushing your teeth.

(Frank Carson)

When I was 60 I said to my wife, "Let's go upstairs and make love." She said, "Darling, I can't do both."

(Noel V. Ginnity)

My doctor did me a big favour when I got to 60. He touched up my X-rays.

(Joey Bishop)

I don't need to tell you my age. I have a bladder that does that for me.

(Stephen Fry at 60)

When I retired from work, they told me time wasn't important anymore. The going away present they gave me was... a watch!

(Bob Hope)

The worst thing anybody
ever said about me is
that I'm 60. Which I am.

(Joan Rivers)

I recently turned 60.
Practically a third of
my life is over.

(Woody Allen)

One of the hardest decisions to make in life is when to start your sixties.

(Zsa Zsa Gabor)

60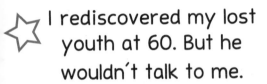

I rediscovered my lost youth at 60. But he wouldn't talk to me.

(Frederick Marx)

When men reach their sixties they retire and go to pieces. Women just go right on cooking.

(Gail Sheehy)

The pleasures that
once were heaven,
look silly at 67.

(Noel Coward)

I'm 60. My `get up and go` has just got up and gone.

(Derek Davis)

I'm 60. I can live without sex, but not without my glasses.

(Fred Perry)

One day when I was 45, I went into the kitchen to make myself a cup of tea. When I came out, I was 68.

(Thora Hird)

60

I'm at the age where
just putting my cigarette
in the holder is a thrill.

(George Burns)

60 ☆

60

☆

☆

☆

My daughter told me
she was in the family
way. I'm 60. I'm in
everybody's bloody way!

(Joe Hanratty)

When a man of 60 runs
off with a young woman,
I wish him luck. After all
he's going to need it.

(Deborah Kerr)

Life begins at 60. But so does arthritis, lumbago, insomnia, amnesia...

(Hal Roach)

They told me my sex drive would improve at 60. Bunkum. When you're 60 you get social security, not girls.

(Neil Simon)

Yes, I admit I'm 60 years of age, but that's only 16 if you do it in Celsius.

(George Carlin)

I tried not to get depressed when I hit 60. I told myself that I was only 59 the day before. Then I put my head in the oven.

(Les Dawson)

When I got to 60, I went to the doctor and told him I was fixated on sex. He said "It's all in your mind." I said "That's the problem!"

(Bob Monkhouse)

60

When I got to 60, I looked in the mirror and said "Who's that old fart?" It certainly wasn't me.

(Dave Allen)

Sex in the twenties - brilliant. Sex in the sixties? "Ouch! My stomach."

(Sandy Lieber)

I'm 62 years old.
That's 85,000 in
 frequent flier miles.

(Barry Kelly)

My wife's most difficult age was 60. It took her 7 years to get out of it.

(Sean Keaveney)

They say the average
man of 60 has spent
over 20 years in bed.
No wonder I don't
feel too tired.

(Tommy Cooper)

When you get to 60
your hair stops growing
on your head and starts
coming out your ears
and your nose instead.
That's how God shows
you he loves you.

(Chris Rock)

I have the body of an 18 year old. I keep it in the fridge.

(Spike Milligan at 60)

One starts to get young at the age of 60. But by then it's too late.

(Pablo Picasso)

The years between 50 and 70 are the hardest. You're always being asked to do things, and you're not yet decrepit enough to turn them down.

 (T.S Eliot)

I'm now in my
sixtieth decade.

(Mort Sahl)

At 60 you have everything you had at 50... except it's all a bit lower.

(Gypsy Rose Lee)

When I got to 60,
I said to my wife,
"Men are like wine.
They improve with
age." She locked
me in the cellar.

(Rodney Dangerfield)

The doctor told me I looked great for a man of 60. It's a pity I'm only 50.

(Les Dawson)

My grandmother started walking five miles a day when she got to 60. She's 97 now, but we don't know where the hell she is.

(Ellen DeGeneres)

60

My wife couldn't wait
to be sixty. She wanted
to get a facelift so she
could look younger.

(Del Shannon)

Since I got to 60, I
look better, feel better
and make love better.
And I also lie better.

(George Burns)

My mother is over 60 but she still doesn't need glasses. Drinks right from the bottle.

(Zero Mostel)

A stockbroker urged me to buy things that would triple in value every year. "At my age," I told him, "I don't even buy green bananas.

(Claude Pepper at 60)

When you get to 60 your
idea of a good night out
is a good night in.

(Terry Wogan)

There's only one cure for grey hair. It was invented by a French man. It's called the guillotine.

(P.G. Wodehouse at 60)

60

Inside every 60 year old is a 30 year old saying "What the fuck just happened?"

(Dave Allen)

I am just turning forty, and taking my time about it.

(Comedian Harold Lloyd after being asked his age when he was 77)

At last my wife admitted she was 60. The problem is, she didn't say when.

(Paul Power)

I asked my wife if I looked 60. She said, "Not anymore honey."

(Henny Youngman)

Sex in the sixties is great. And it gets even better if you pull over to the side of the road.

(Johnny Carson)

After a man passes 60 his mischief is mainly in his head.

(Edgar Watson Howe)

At 60, work is a lot less fun
and fun is a lot more work.

(Maureen Potter)

My wife is approaching 60, but she won't say from which direction.

(Bob Hope)

Fred Davis, the doyen of snooker, is now 67 years of age and too old to get his leg over. He prefers to use his left hand.

(Ted Lowe)

The doctor said to me,
"You're going to live
till you're 60." I said,
"I AM 60!" He said,
"What did I tell you?"

(Henny Youngman)

I stopped playing James Bond when the villians started to be younger than me.

(Roger Moore at 63)

I refuse to retire.
I'm useless at
crossword puzzles.

(Norman Mailer)

I considered retiring at 60, but now I'm too old.

(George Burns at 67)

When you get to 60 you lose interest in sex, your friends drift away and your children ignore you. There are other advantages too.

(Richard Needham)

I told my wife I was going to retire when I could no longer hear the sound of laughter. She said, "That never stopped you before."

(Bob Hope)

The only whistles I
get these days are
from kettles.

(Racquel Welch at 63)

Just keep pissing in your pyjamas and complaining about everything. That's the great benefit of old age.

(Eric Idle)

I'm 60, the age at which you go upstairs, stop on the middle step and say to yourself, "What did I come up here for?"

(Derek Davis)

60 60

Age is only a number. In my case, quite a large number.

(Woody Allen at 69)

She claims she just
turned 30. It must
have been a U-turn.

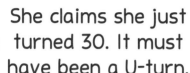

Allow me to put the record straight. I'm 46 and have been for some years past.

(Erica Jong)

An archaeologist is the best husband any woman can have. The older she gets, the more interested he is in her.

(Agatha Christie)

☆

A sixty year old man asks his younger wife,"Will you love me when I'm old and grey?" To which she replies, "I do."

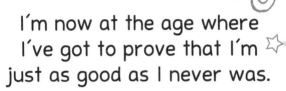

I'm now at the age where I've got to prove that I'm just as good as I never was.

(Rex Harrison)

I'm at the age where
my back goes out
more than I do.

(Phyllis Diller)

I'm pushing 60.
That's exercise
enough for anyone.

(Mark Twain)

You know you're getting older when you try to straighten out the wrinkles in your socks, and discover you're not wearing any.

(Leonard Knott)

At my age, the only reason I'd take up jogging again would be to hear heavy breathing.

(Erma Bombeck)

I refuse to admit I'm more than 52, even if that makes my sons illegitimate.

(Nancy Astor)

I wish I could tell
you my age but it's
impossible. It keeps
changing all the time.

(Greer Garson)

I've just retired. My boss
doesn't appreciate me.
He said, "We're not losing
a worker, we're gaining
a parking space."

(Rodney Dangerfield)

You know you're getting old when everything hurts. And what doesn't hurt doesn't work.

(Hy Gardner)

60 60

I've often been asked to what do I attribute my great age. I always say, "To the fact that I was born a long time ago."

(Spike Milligan)

I'm at the age
where, if a girl says
no, I'm grateful.

(Bob Hope at 68)

Will you still need me,
Will you still feed me,
When I'm 64?

(Lennon/McCartney)